DEPARTURES

The Lee family is on holiday.

Bye!

Thanks.

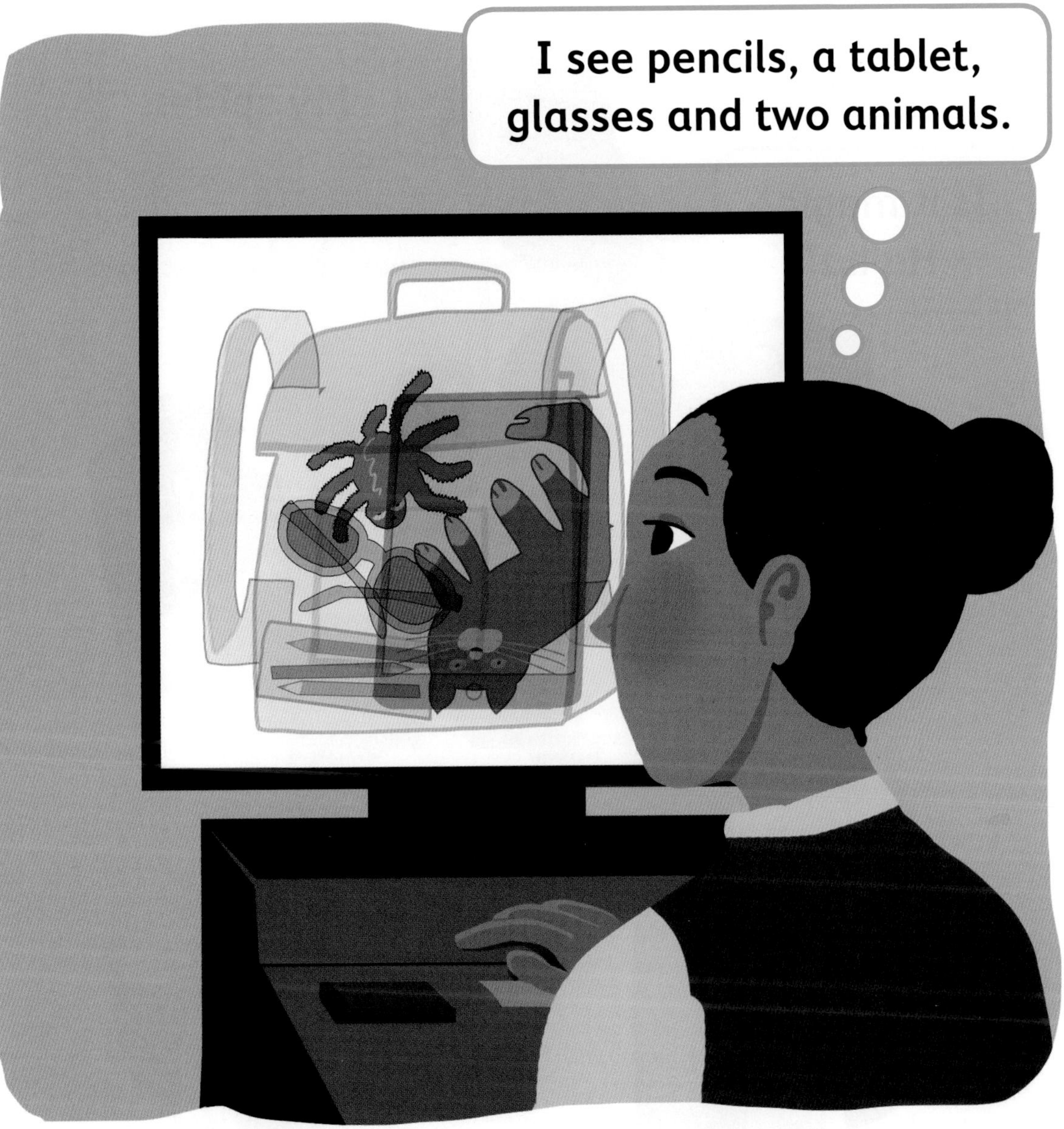
I see pencils, a tablet, glasses and two animals.

5

Amy likes the game on her tablet. Sam reads.

They sleep now.

Are the toys in the bag?

No.

The spider looks at the glasses.
He likes them.

The toys run.

MAGIC!

Amy and Sam
look at the tablet.

14

Activities

Before You Read

1 **Look at page 1. Say or write Yes (Y) or No (N).**

1 The family is on holiday. ☐   **4** The boy has got a red bag. ☐
2 They have got ten bags. ☐   **5** The girl is sad. ☐
3 There is a boy and a girl. ☐

After You Read

1 **Put the right word in the sentences.**

> sleep   magic   tablet   glasses

1 The toys in the yellow bag are _____ .
2 Where are Mr Barker's _____ ?
  The spider has got them on his face.
3 At home Amy and Sam _____ in a bed.
4 The cat plays with the _____ .

2 **Put the pictures in the right order.**

ⓐ ☐   ⓑ ☐   ⓒ ☐
ⓓ ☐   ⓔ ☐   ⓕ ☐

Pearson Education Limited
Edinburgh Gate, Harlow,
Essex CM20 2JE, England
and Associated Companies throughout the world.

ISBN: 978-1-4082-8824-5

This edition first published by Pearson Education Ltd 2014

13

Set in 19/23pt OT Fiendstar Semibold
Printed in China
SWTC/13

Illustrations: Galia Bernstein (nb illustration)

Published by Pearson Education Ltd.

For a complete list of the titles available in the Pearson English Kids Readers series, please go to
www.pearsonenglishkidsreaders.com. Alternatively, write to your local Pearson Education office or to
Pearson English Readers Marketing Department, Pearson Education, Edinburgh Gate, Harlow, Essex CM20 2JE, England.